VOLCANOES
By Ruth Radlauer

A Radlauer Geo Book

AN ELK GROVE BOOK

 CHILDRENS PRESS, CHICAGO

For help with the manuscript, the author thanks Mr. Dale C. Thompson, Mount Rainier National Park.

Maps and diagrams by Rolf Zillmer

Photographs:
Eldon D. Anderson/Dale Steininger, cover, page 16
Cheryl Haselhorst, THE COLUMBIAN, Vancouver, Washington, pages 4, 6, 38
National Park Service, pages 10, 12, 26, 30
National Park Service, Alaska Area Office
 Bob Nichols, page 24
 Keith Trexler, page 24
Richard L. Shaw, page 28
Rolf Zillmer, page 32

Cover:
Mount St. Helens, March 30, 1980
—By Eldon D. Andersen/Dale Steininger

Library of Congress Cataloging in Publication Data

Radlauer, Ruth Shaw.
 Volcanoes.
 "A Radlauer geo book."
 "An Elk Grove book."
 Includes index.
 SUMMARY: Discusses volcanoes and the way they erupt, specifically a number of North American ones, especially Mount Saint Helens.
 1. Volcanoes—Juvenile literature. [1. Volcanoes]
 I. Title.
 QE521.3.R32   551.2'1   80-24564
 ISBN 0-516-07835-6

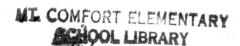

CONTENTS

On May 18, 1980, a mountain "blew its top."

MOUNT SAINT HELENS

     Mount Saint Helens, a **dormant** volcano in the state of Washington, started to tremble on March 20, 1980. **Volcanologists** rushed to St. Helens to study and measure. Using instruments, they measured how much the mountainside was swelling and how much it quaked. Hot gases and **magma,** moving within a volcano, make it swell and quake.

     This dormant volcano had not **erupted** since 1857, but the volcanologists said Mount St. Helens could "blow her top" at any time.

     Eight weeks later, Mount St. Helens erupted with a force many times as great as the first atom bomb dropped in World War II.

dormant
     "asleep," quiet, inactive

volcanologist
     scientist who studies volcanoes

magma
     hot, liquid rock under the earth's surface

erupt
     to come out with force; in a volcano, to spout or throw out lava, gas, ash, or cinder

"I used to love Mount St. Helens, but look
what she's done. I hate her! I hate her!"

I HATE HER!

It was something that couldn't happen. A beautiful, snow-capped mountain where people fished, hiked, and camped wouldn't blow up. It wouldn't destroy animals, trees, and homes. But it did.

Before the big blast, heat and fumes poured out for weeks. **Glaciers** and snow melted, sending water and mud into Spirit Lake at the base of St. Helens.

Finally, on the morning of May 18, the north side of the peak turned to mush and slid down in an **avalanche.** This was almost like uncapping a bottle of soda pop that's been shaken. The avalanche "uncorked" all the heat and gas within the volcano. It exploded with a boom heard 200 miles away. A cloud of **ash** and steam climbed twelve miles into the sky above the mountain. Mount St. Helens had awakened with a roar.

glacier
> a large body of ice formed by years of snow pile-up that packs and turns to ice

avalanche
> large mass of earth, snow, and rocks that moves suddenly down a slope

ash
> very fine, powdery particles of magma or lava

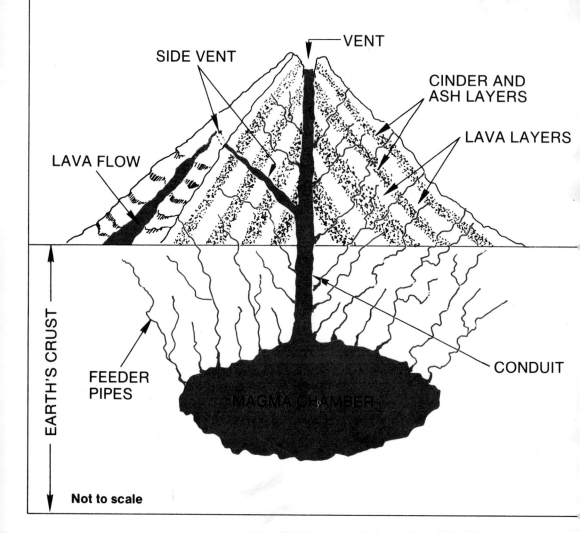

STRATOVOLCANO

VENT

SIDE VENT

CINDER AND
ASH LAYERS

LAVA LAYERS

LAVA FLOW

EARTH'S CRUST

CONDUIT

FEEDER
PIPES

MAGMA CHAMBER

Not to scale

Melted rock, or magma, wells up through
cracks in the earth. It passes up the conduit
and gushes out of the side or top vent.

WHAT IS A VOLCANO?

A volcano is a hole where melted rock called magma or rock and ash are thrown up from inside the earth. The mountain formed by many layers of cooled **lava** is also called a volcano.

When magma gets hot enough and full of gases, it flows toward cracks or holes in the **earth's crust.** Sometimes the magma flows into a **conduit,** or "pipe," and comes out the top of the volcano. Or it may burst through cracks in the side called **fissures.**

But where does this red hot, liquid rock come from? And how does it get so hot?

lava
    melted rock; magma at or near the surface
earth's crust
    the outer layer of the earth, about 20 miles thick under land and three miles thick under ocean basins
conduit
    the main passageway or "pipe" that reaches from deep in the earth to the top of a volcano
fissure
    crack, also called a rift

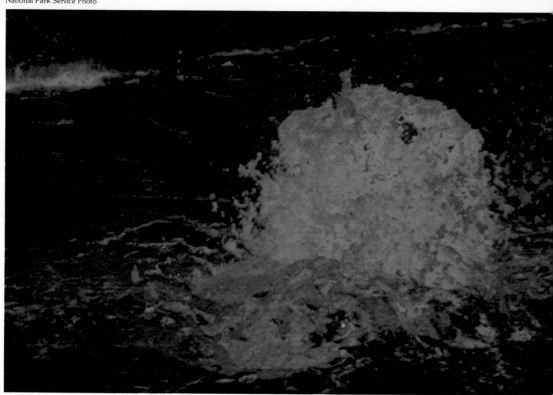

Lava flows from the magma chamber
beneath the Pacific Plate and creates islands
like Hawaii.

THE MAKING OF MAGMA

Scientists believe the center of the earth is very hot. Around the earth's center, or **core,** is a **mantle** of solid rock. A crust 10 to 25 miles thick covers the mantle.

The mantle is hot enough to melt, but under weight and pressure it remains solid. If the crust cracks, pressure is taken off and some of the mantle melts. Molten rock then collects in **magma chambers** or finds its way to the surface.

Scientists think the earth's crust is like a cracked shell on a boiled egg. Each broken piece of crust is called a **plate**. All of these huge plates drift very slowly. In the Pacific Ocean, a plate has moved over a "hot spot," or magma chamber, for millions of years. Many islands were formed by volcanoes that erupted through the Pacific Plate as it passed over the hot spot. Some of those islands are the Hawaiian Islands.

core
> center of the earth—The inner core and outer core together are about 4400 miles across

mantle
> hot, solid layer of rock about 1800 miles thick surrounding the core

magma chambers
> spaces within the earth where magma collects

plate
> section of earth's crust

Pahoehoe lava flows often on the island of Hawaii. Magma is hot liquid rock within the earth's crust. Lava is hot liquid rock at or close to the earth's surface

MAGMA AND LAVA

Magma often rises close to the surface of the earth without erupting as a volcano. There it hardens and becomes **granite, syenite,** and other kinds of rock. If the earth rises and soil washes away, or **erodes**, big granite rocks are left uncovered.

When magma shoots to the earth's surface, it becomes the lava of a volcano. Lava takes many forms. If it is smooth and liquid, volcanologists call it **pahoehoe.** If it is chunky and rough, it's **aa.**

Sometimes lava clings to a tree and burns it up. If the outer part of the lava cools while the tree is burning up inside, a **lava tree** is left standing like a grizzly ghost.

granite
   rock formed when magma hardens within the earth's crust
syenite
   another kind of rock formed when magma hardens beneath the surface
erode
   to wash or wear away
pahoehoe
   smooth or ropy lava
aa
   chunky, rough lava
lava tree
   hardened lava shaped like a tree

Haleakala on the island of Maui in
Hawaii is the place to see bombs, lapilli,
tears, cinder, and cinder cones.

BOMBS, TEARS, AND CINDER

A volcano may throw out blobs of lava bigger than baseballs. If these **ejecta** harden before they hit the earth, they're called **bombs.** Smaller hardened blobs are called **lapilli.** Sometimes the lapilli take the shape of droplets called **Pele's tears.** Pele is the Hawaiian volcano goddess of fire. **Pele's hair** is volcanic glass spun out by the wind to look like hair.

Lava may be frothy as it shoots into the air. Gases bursting from gobs of lava turn them into bits that look like pieces of sponge. They harden into **cinder** about the size of peas or grapes. Cinder is heavier than smaller bits blown away by the wind. It often falls back down close to the volcano and forms a **cinder cone** around the **vent.**

ejecta
> rock thrown out by volcanic explosions

bombs
> ejecta larger than 1½ inches across

lapilli
> ejecta smaller than 1½ inches across

Pele's tears
> lapilli shaped like tears

Pele's hair
> volcanic glass spun out by wind into fine strands

cinder
> spongelike bits of lava the size of peas or grapes

cinder cone
> cone-shaped hill of cinder

vent
> hole through which volcano erupts

On April 12, 1980, Mount St. Helens
looked peacefully down on farms and foothills.

KINDS OF VOLCANOES

The Klickitat Indians called Mount St. Helens *Tah-one-lat-clah,* Fire Mountain. Scientists call it a **pyroclastic volcano** and a **stratovolcano.** Before the 1980 eruptions, St. Helens had steep, even sides. When it erupted long ago, it tossed up cinder and bombs that fell back down around the vent. Ejecta piled up and made a cone. Later, these ejecta were covered with lava. When a volcano builds up layers of cinder and layers of lava, it's called a stratovolcano, because *strata* means layers. It's also called a **composite volcano.**

Mount St. Helens has been called the Northwest's most explosive volcano. It's been known as the Fujiyama of America because it looks so much like that famous volcano in Japan. But no matter what you call it, St. Helen's peak is no longer 9,677 feet high. In June of 1980, the mountain measured about 8,400 feet.

pyroclastic volcano
    fairly steep-sided, cone-shaped volcano made up of cinder
    and other large ejecta
stratovolcano
    one made up of layers
composite volcano
    volcano made up of a mixture of kinds of layers

The Hawaiian Islands are made of lava.
Their volcanoes are domelike with gentle,
sloping sides. This is Mauna Loa on the big
island of Hawaii.

SHIELD VOLCANOES

Volcanoes in Hawaii are not as dangerous as some in other parts of the world. Their lava is very liquid with a lower content of gas, so they erupt with less force. Because the lava builds a mound shaped like a shield, these are called **shield volcanoes.**

Lava flows are hot enough to burn up trees and anything else in their paths. But with care they can be studied. During quiet periods, volcanologists place instruments all around the volcanoes. Electric signals travel from the instruments to the **observatory** near the **crater** of Kilauea. The instruments show how much and where the earth is swelling and quaking. Scientists can sometimes tell where a volcano might erupt.

They get ready to take pictures and gather samples of lava. Roads and trails are closed. And sometimes a place is provided where visitors can view the "fireworks" in safety.

shield volcano
mound-shaped volcano
observatory
building where scientists observe, or watch, and study
crater
a bowl or basin around the opening of a volcano

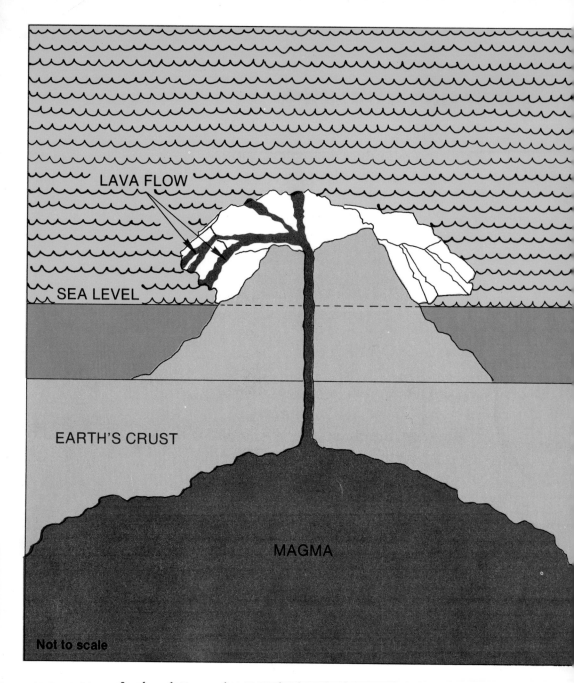

LAVA FLOW

SEA LEVEL

EARTH'S CRUST

MAGMA

Not to scale

Iceland is made up of islands formed by volcanoes. Lava erupts along fissures created when plates pull apart beneath the Atlantic Ocean.

FISSURE ERUPTIONS

Under the Atlantic Ocean, volcanoes formed in another way. Here plates have been pulling away from each other for millions of years. As the plates move, they crack. This takes pressure off the magma which then rises to the surface in a volcanic eruption.

These are called **fissure eruptions.** They come up in huge masses many miles long. An island country, Iceland, was formed by fissure or **Icelandic eruptions.** Formation of this country began millions of years ago, but its main volcano, Hekla, is still active. A new volcanic island, Surtsey, was born south of Iceland in 1963. An eruption in 1976 created the island of Eldfell.

fissure eruption
    magma rising from a large crack in the earth's crust
Icelandic eruption
    another name for fissure eruption

A volcano often has a crater or caldera
at its top. Visitors can hike across the crater
of Kilauea Iki in Hawaii.

CRATERS AND CALDERAS

A crater is like a bowl around the vent, or hole, where a volcano erupts. Some craters are formed by explosion. Others form when the top of the volcano sinks or collapses.

If a crater is wider across than one mile, it's called a **caldera.** At times, a volcano erupts and makes a crater within its caldera.

In Hawaii Volcanoes National Park, you can walk across a crater. Kilauea Iki, which erupted in 1959, is still steaming. Magma under the crater heats rainwater that flows through the cracks in the hardened lava. The water boils and turns to steam which rises like wispy ghosts.

caldera
   a volcanic crater that is wider than one mile or 1.6 kilometers across

An eruption in 1912 made a huge
caldera in the top of Alaska's Katmai. Six
miles away a new volcano was created:
Novarupta. Katmai erupted again in 1931.

KATMAI

More than 50 volcanoes dot the map of Alaska. Forty of them have erupted since 1700. The famous Katmai erupted in 1912, but exactly what happened was a mystery for some time. Later studies told the story.

Just before the eruption, a valley below the moutain broke open in many places and magma poured through the cracks, or fissures. Great rivers of lava drained out of Katmai through an underground passageway and came out of a smaller volcano, Novarupta, six miles away. One thousand feet lower than Katmai, Novarupta acted as an escape valve. When Katmai lost this huge store of magma, it could no longer support its own weight. The top of Katmai collapsed and formed a caldera over 1½ miles deep and more than three miles across. Today a lake fills the caldera.

For a long time the valley was full of steam vents, or **fumaroles.** It was named The Valley of Ten Thousand Smokes.

fumarole
  opening where steam and gases come out, usually in craters of dormat volcanoes or near them

About 75,000 years ago, Mount Rainier
was around 16,000 feet high. But glaciers
and erosion cut it down to its present size.
At 14,410 feet, Mount Rainier is the highest
peak in the Cascade Range.

THE CASCADES

Millions of years ago, fissure eruptions spilled lava over a wide area of Washington and Oregon. This huge bed of lava is now called the Columbia River Plateau.

In this same part of the country, many, many years later, the Juan de Fuca Plate pushed very slowly under the American Plate. Today these plates are still pushing against each other. Their movement makes the earth buckle and form mountains. It also causes earthquakes and volcanoes.

As the plates rub together, they get very hot. Sometimes they crack. When the earth's crust cracks, it takes off some of the pressure that keeps the mantle from melting.

Over many thousands of years, a little at a time, the American Plate cracked along the edge. In places along these cracks, magma welled up to create 15 volcanoes now called the **Cascade Range.**

Cascade Range
   volcanic mountains in British Columbia, Canada, Washington, Oregon, and California

Another volcanic mountain of the
Cascade Range was Mount Mazama.
Crater Lake fills its caldera.

MOUNT MAZAMA

Scientists can only guess about Mount Mazama. A few million years ago, this volcano spewed out ash and cinder. Then lava flowed down its sides. For many centuries, the mountain grew in an endless cycle of ash and cinder eruptions between layers of lava flows.

Then Mount Mazama rested through the Ice Age. After the glaciers melted, flowers and trees began to grow on the mountainsides.

Finally, about 6,500 years ago, a series of mighty blasts blew the peak off Mount Mazama. The top of the volcano collapsed and formed a tremendous caldera.

As if exhausted, the volcano was quiet for a long time. Then it belched once more and created a cone within the caldera.

Today, rain water has filled part of the caldera to form the deepest lake in the United States. Now known as Crater Lake, it is six miles across and 2000 feet deep. And rising above the lake near the north shore is the volcanic cone called Wizard Island.

In Lassen Volcanic National Park is
another Cascade Range volcano, Lassen Peak.

LASSEN PEAK

California's Lassen Peak is a very old volcanic **dome.** It formed during the Ice Age on the side of a much larger stratovolcano known as Brokeoff Volcano or old Mount Tehama.

Quiet since 1850, this Cascade volcano surprised everyone in 1914. On May 22, a black cloud erupted into the afternoon sky and began a show of "fireworks" that lit up the sky, off and on, for seven years.

Today, in Lassen Volcanic National Park, visitors can see hot springs, steam vents called fumaroles, four craters, a cinder cone, and piles of lava.

Will Lassen erupt again? It's hard to say, but when you look at the records of Cascade Range eruptions, you find many of them erupted during the middle of the 1800s. Could that mean more volcanoes in the group will erupt in the 1980s? Perhaps you should ask a volcanologist.

dome
   lava that piles up around a vent when it's too thick to flow

In July of 1980, instruments recorded
movements beneath Mount Hood, 60 miles
from Mount Saint Helens.

MOUNT HOOD

Another volcano in the Cascade Range, Mount Hood, has been dormant since about 1865. Before that time, in about 1803, this Oregon state volcano erupted violently and built a six-inch layer of ash on one side of the vent.

Later, between 1846 and 1865, Mount Hood grumbled and gave off fiery flashes. Mount St. Helens erupted during some of those years, so you might wonder if these two volcanoes tend to erupt at about the same time.

In 1980, almost two months after the new activity around St. Helens, Mount Hood began to stir. For two days, about 160 earthquakes beneath Mount Hood made the **seismograph** needle jump. Was Mount Hood about to erupt?

Of the 300 earthquakes recorded that week, many could have been caused by dynamite set off by lumbermen removing tree stumps. The rest of the quakes were thought to be readjustments and settling of the earth in that area. It's almost as if this dormant volcano "snored in its sleep."

People in Oregon and Washington probably look up at Mount Hood, Mount Rainier, and other Cascade Range volcanoes and wonder, "What's next?"

seismograph
> instrument that records earth movements—A needle marks these movements on a turning drum.

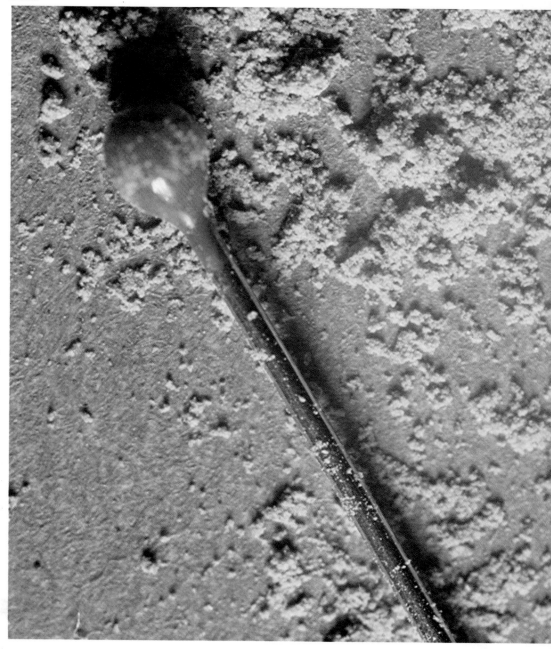

On May 18, 1980, Mount St. Helens hurled ash and steam 12 miles into the sky. The ash cloud traveled east. Each of the following big eruptions sent an ash cloud in a different direction. (Magnified ash is shown here with a common pin.)

ASH

When a volcano explodes, it throws clouds of steam and lava into the air. Much of the lava cools and hardens as it flies up. Heavy pieces, cinders, bombs, and lapilli, fall near the volcano. Tiny bits called ash are carried ever higher by the heat and blown hundreds of miles away by winds.

After Mount St. Helens erupted on May 18, ash fell on Washington, Idaho, Montana and other states. Highways and city streets had to be cleared of a blanket of "gray snow." The ash, which was like powdered glass, caused machinery to break down. Schools were closed, and people stayed inside to keep from breathing the ash into their lungs. Those who did go outside wore special masks to **filter** the air.

Airliners were damaged when they flew through some of the ash. A high-altitude ash cloud could circle the earth for a year or more.

filter
> to keep ash particles out of the air you breath by using a mask

Pahoehoe lava flows over living things
on the big island of Hawaii. It leaves
devastation in its path.

DEVASTATION

The eruption of St. Helens caused mudflows that clogged two branches of the Toutle River and buried a vacation spot at nearby Spirit Lake. It killed over 30 people, knocked down bridges, and blew over a forest. The volcano "turned day into night" when it dumped a cloud of ash on Yakima, Washington, 85 miles to the east.

From the air, a rescue pilot said, "Trees and all the vegetation are laid out flat, singed, burned, sizzling." Another reported, ". . . a flow of white, burning everything it touches."

Devastation is a volcano's follower. But where volcanoes are studied, measured, and watched, as in Hawaii, people get warnings. They usually don't build houses where lava might flow.

Still, volcanoes are full of surprises. It's hard to predict what they'll do. In 1980, no one really believed Washington's St. Helens would erupt. That was something that happened centuries ago, or maybe only in faraway places.

Many houses, barns, trucks, and cars
were flooded or almost buried in mud after
St. Helens erupted May 18, 1980.

THE MUCK IS COMING!

As soon as St. Helens stirred in March of that year, many people did get ready. When the blast came, alerted helicopter pilots rescued 125 people from danger. A telephone "ring down" warned 3000 people living around the volcano to get out, or **evacuate.** Each person who received a warning telephoned two others until most people knew they must evacuate.

Modern "Paul Reveres" in sheriff's cars used bullhorns as they drove through danger zones calling, "Evacuate! Evacuate! The muck is coming!" Muck was a mixture of mud and hot gases.

Some refused to leave their homes until they learned that poison gas was coming along with the mud.

From that day on, folks had a new respect for Mount St. Helens and all the other Cascade Range volcanoes.

evacuate
    to leave a home or building, especially in a time and area
    of danger

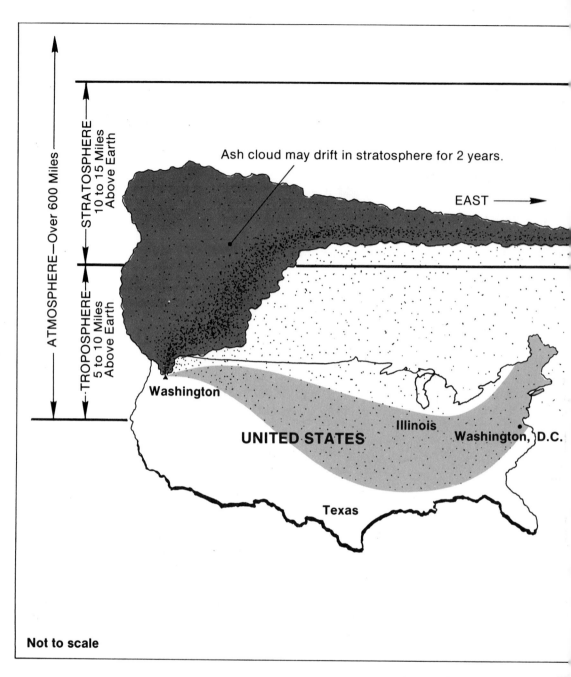

Ash cloud may drift in stratosphere for 2 years.

EAST →

ATMOSPHERE—Over 600 Miles

STRATOSPHERE
10 to 15 Miles
Above Earth

TROPOSPHERE
5 to 10 Miles
Above Earth

Washington

UNITED STATES

Illinois

Washington, D.C.

Texas

Not to scale

No one is sure what effects the volcano
will have on future weather.

WEATHER EFFECTS

The whole world can be affected by a volcano. The cloud of ash that rises high into the **atmosphere** often drifts around the earth for two years or more. Acting like a sunshade, the dust in the upper atmosphere absorbs sunlight and also reflects it back into space. In 1816, a much dustier cloud from Mount Tambora in the Dutch East Indies caused June snowfalls and mid-summer frosts halfway around the world in New England.

Some **climatologists** think perhaps St. Helens' cloud will bring only slightly cooler temperatures. But other climatologists say bigger changes may come about.

Meteorologists say the shade of the dust cloud will cool the earth. This will reduce the number of thunderstorms which are produced by rising ground heat. On the other hand, the dust might **seed the clouds** and produce more rain than usual.

atmosphere
mass of air surrounding the earth
climatologist
one who studies the forces that create climate
meteorologist
scientist who studies the atmosphere and what happens to it, especially the weather it produces
seed the clouds
to give the moisture in rainclouds solid particles on which to form droplets heavy enough to fall as rain

Plants like this kupukupu fern are the
first "pioneers" to settle and grow in
Hawaiian lava.

THE BRIGHTER SIDE

There is a bright side to the story of Mount St. Helens. Scientists now have a new **"laboratory."** As St. Helens erupts again and again, they can measure, study, and learn more about volcanoes and their effects.

And other people have made the best of a bad thing. They've sold T-shirts that read, "I survived Mount St. Helens" or "I lava volcano." One company made an ash filter mask with a smile on it and the words, "Grin and bear it."

In the future, the area may be a tourist attraction. It could even become a national park.

And just as rainstorms can bring rainbows, violent volcanoes can bring good soil. Volcanic ash adds minerals to crop lands. Even where lava flows, plants can take root and grow. Their roots break down big chunks of lava and turn it into sand. The plants die, decay, and add **nutrients.** Then other plants can grow. Slowly, lava turns to rich new soil. Devastation is forgotten as new life begins.

laboratory
    a place where you can experiment and study
nutrient
    a substance that feeds and helps things grow

GLOSSARY

aa
> chunky, rough lava; from Hawaiian

ash
> very fine, powdery bits of lava, less than one tenth of an inch (less than 4 mm) across

ash flow
> mixture of hot gas and rock about the size of ash, exploding from a crater or fissure

atmosphere
> mass of air surrounding the earth, composed of lower troposphere and upper stratosphere

avalanche
> large mass of earth, snow, or rocks that moves suddenly down a slope

block
> angular chunk of rock ejected during an eruption

bombs
> ejecta larger than 1½ inches across

caldera
> a volcanic crater that is wider than one mile or 1.6 kilometers across

Cascade Range
> a chain of volcanic mountains created by the movement of the Juan de Fuca Plate under the North American Plate; includes Mt. Garibaldi in British Columbia, Canada; Mt. Baker, Glacier Peak, Mt. Rainier, Mt. Adams, Mt. St. Helens in Washington; Mt. Hood, Mt. Jefferson, Three Sisters, Mt. Thielsen, Crater Lake (Mt. Mazama), Mt. McLoughlin in Oregon; Mt. Shasta, Lassen Peak in California

cinder
> spongelike bits of lava the size of peas or grapes—The holes in cinder are made by escaping gases as the lava hardens, usually as it erupts.

cinder cone
> cone-shaped hill or mountain of cinder piled up around the vent of a volcano—Most cinder cones have steep, even sides, and a crater at the top.

climatologist
> a scientist who studies the atmosphere and what happens to it, especially the weather it produces

composite volcano
    volcano made up of a mixture of kinds of layers—They
    are often made of alternate layers of lava and pyroclastic
    material.

conduit
    the main passageway or "pipe" that reaches from the
    magma chamber deep in the earth to the top of a volcano

core
    center of the earth—The inner core is thought to be solid
    and mostly iron. The outer core is liquid. Together, the
    inner and outer core are about 4400 miles across.

crater
    a bowl or basin around the opening of a volcano formed
    by explosion or collapse of the top of the volcano

dome
    lava that piles up around a vent when the lava is too thick
    to flow

dormant
    "asleep," quiet, inactive

earth's crust
    the outer layer of the earth, about 10 to 25 miles thick
    under land, or continents, and about three miles thick
    under ocean basins

ejecta
    rock thrown out by volcanic explosions

erode
    to wash or wear away

erupt
    to come out with force; in a volcano to spout or throw
    out lava, gas, ash, or cinder

evacuate
    to leave a home or building, especially in a time and area
    of danger

filter
    to keep ash particles out of the air you breathe by
    using a mask

fissure
    crack, also called a rift

fumarole

opening where steam and gases come out usually in craters of dormant volcanoes, often near volcanoes

glacier

a large body of ice formed by years of snow pile-up that packs and turns to ice

granite

one of several kinds of rock formed when magma hardens within the earth's crust

Icelandic eruption

another name for fissure eruption; magma rising from a large crack in the earth's crust

laboratory

a place where students and scientists can experiment and study

lapilli

ejecta smaller than 1½ inches across

lava

melted rock; magma at or near the earth's surface

lava tree

hardened lava shaped like a tree, formed when lava clings to a tree and hardens—The tree is usually burned up inside the lava formation.

lava tube

tube formed inside a lava flow

magma

hot, liquid rock under the earth's surface—When magma comes to the surface, it's called lava.

magma chamber

space within the earth where magma collects

mantle

hot, solid layer of rock about 1800 miles thick surrounding the core of the earth

meteorologist

scientist who studies the atmosphere and what happens to it—They usually try to predict weather.

nutrient

a substance that feeds and helps things grow

observatory

a building where scientists observe, or watch, and study

pahoehoe

smooth or ropy lava; from Hawaiian

Pele

the Hawaiian goddess of fire—Legend says she creates volcanoes where she can live and be safe from her cruel sister, Na Maka o Kahai, goddess of the sea.

Pele's hair
 volcanic glass spun out by wind into fine strands

Pele's tears
 lapilli shaped like tears

plate
 a huge section of the earth's crust

pyroclastic flow
 movement of hot gas and rock fragments from a volcano

pyroclastic volcano
 fairly steep-sided, cone-shaped volcano made up of cinder
 and other large ejecta

seed the clouds
 to give the moisture in rainclouds solid particles on which
 to form droplets big and heavy enough to fall as rain

seismograph
 instrument that records earth movements—A needle
 marks these movements on a turning cylinder, or drum.

shield volcano
 mound-shaped volcano made mostly of lava flows; so
 named because it looks like a shield lying down with the
 curved side up

steam vent
 see *fumarole*

strata
 layers

stratosphere
 the upper part of the atmosphere

stratovolcano
 a volcano made up of layers, often alternating layers of
 lava and pyroclastic flows

syenite
 one of several kinds of rock formed when magma hardens
 beneath the earth's surface

tree mold
 a hollow impression of a tree left in cooled, hardened lava
 after it has surrounded and burned up a tree

troposphere
 lower part of the atmosphere

vent
 hole through which a volcano erupts

volcanologist
 scientist who studies volcanoes

Vulcan
 Roman god of fire and metal works

INDEX